I've Got Tears in My Ears
from Lyin' on My Back in My Bed While I Cry Over You

Country Music's Best (and Funniest) Lines

Compiled by Paula Schwed

Andrews and McMeel
A Universal Press Syndicate Company
Kansas City

Designed and illustrated by Gary Britt

Library of Congress Cataloging-in-Publication Data
I've got tears in my ears from lyin' on my back in bed while I cry
    over you : country music's best (and funniest) lines / compiled by
Paula Schwed.
        p. cm.
    ISBN 0-8362-7999-9 (ppb.) : $6.95
    1. Country music—Texts.   I. Schwed, Paula.
ML54.6.19   1992 <Case>
782.42164 '2' 0268—dc20   92-5587
                                                              CIP
                                                              MN

ATTENTION: SCHOOLS AND BUSINESSES

Introduction

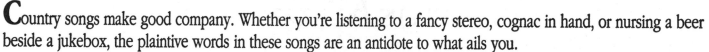

Country songs make good company. Whether you're listening to a fancy stereo, cognac in hand, or nursing a beer beside a jukebox, the plaintive words in these songs are an antidote to what ails you.

The lines resonate with the ache of lost love, the shame of straying, the fury over a double-cross. They celebrate the wonder of brand-new romance and take a good-natured poke at fickle partners.

I learned to love country music as a raw recruit to journalism in 1976, arriving in Nashville without knowing a soul, to work as a reporter for United Press International. As if being a Yankee wasn't bad enough, I was born and reared in New York City, and did not know Dolly Parton from Tammy Wynette. I began to listen, and what appealed to me were the poetry and the farce I heard in the words of country songs.

I believe that's why country music has universal appeal, from President Bush humming along in his office at the White House to the farmer tuning in to the radio while slopping the hogs. It's no-holds-barred emotion that the words evoke, and somehow that makes everyone feel better.

— *PAULA SCHWED*

*For Matt, who never understood
my fascination with country music,
but always believed in me.*

"You must think my bed's a bus stop, the way you come and go"

— From: *Standing room only*, Susan Manchester, Charles Silver, © 1975, 1976 Chappell & Co.,
Sunbury-Music Inc., and World Song Publishing Inc. All rights reserved. Used by permission.

"He even woke me up to say goodbye"

— Mickey Newbury and Doug Gilmore,
Acuff-Rose Music, Inc., 1969.

*Reached No. 2 when recorded in 1969 by Jerry Lee
Lewis for Smash Records.*

"I bought the shoes that just walked out on me"

— Steve Stone and Joe Simpson, Central Songs Inc., 1969.

"If you're going to do me wrong, do it right"

— Max D. Barnes and Vern Gosdin, Blue Lake Music, Hookit Music and Hookem Music, 1983.

Reached No. 5 when recorded in 1983 by Vern Gosdin for Compleat Records.

"I wouldn't take her to a dogfight, even if I thought she could win"

—From: *I wouldn't take her to a dogfight*, Larry Kingston and Troy Snow, © 1967 Careers-BMG Music Publishing, Inc. Used by permission. All rights reserved.

"Flushed from the bathroom of your heart"

—Jack Clement, Songs of Polygram
International, Inc., 1967.

"Who's gonna take your garbage out when I've packed my bags and gone?"

—John C. Tillotson, Thurman T. Wilburn and Lucille Tillotson, Ridge Music Corporation, 1969.

Reached No. 18 when recorded in 1969 by Ernest Tubb and Loretta Lynn for Decca Records.

"You're out doing what I'm here doing without"

— Allen Frizzell and Anthony Roberts, Desert Rose Music and Ski Slope Music, 1983.

"Does my ring hurt your finger when you go out at night?"

—From: *Does my ring hurt your finger,*
  Jan Crutchfield, © Duchess Music Inc., 1967.

"Leaving you is easier than wishing you were gone"

—Joe Douglas, 1980.

"I don't want no more of the cheese, I just want out of the trap"

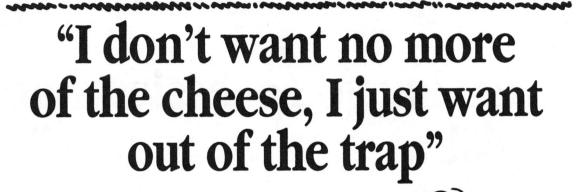

— Glenn Barber, Acuff-Rose Music Inc., 1968.

"I'd rather be picked up here than be put down at home"

— Geoffrey Morgan, Songs of Polygram International Inc., 1975.

"Don't pay the ransom, honey, I've escaped"

—From: *Don't pay the ransom,* Jack Shoemake and Dalton Roberts, © 1972 Cedarwood Publishing.

"You're so cold, I'm turning blue"

— Harlan Howard and Don Davis, Tree Publishing Co. Inc., 1967.
Reached No. 38 when recorded in 1967 by Hugh X. Lewis for Kapp Records.

"Your wife is cheatin' on us again"

— Wayne Kemp and Warren Robb, Tree Publishing Co. Inc. and Screen Gems–EMI Music Inc., 1981.

Reached No. 35 when recorded in 1981 by Wayne Kemp for Mercury Records.

"Hello Mexico, and adios, baby, to you"

— Steve Davis, Billy Sherrill and Glenn Sutton, Algee Music Company, Talbot Music Publishing and Peermusic Ltd., 1978.

"Why have you left the one you left me for?"

— Christopher M. True, Colgems
EMI Music Inc., 1978.
*Reached No. 1 when recorded
in 1978 by Crystal Gayle for
United Artists Records.*

"You changed everything about me but my name"

—Jeannie Seely and Hank Cochran, Tree Publishing Co. Inc., 1967.
Reached No. 35 when recorded in 1968 by Norma Jean for RCA Records.

"She got the goldmine,
I got the shaft"

— Tim Dubois, Warner House of Music, 1983.

"You're a hard dog to keep under the porch"

— Susanna Clark and Harlan Howard, EMI April Music Inc. and Weeping Willow Music, 1984.

"If you don't quit checkin' on me, I'm checkin' out on you"

— Larry Cheshier and Murray Kellum, Talbot Music Publishing Inc., Cary and Mr. Wilson Music, Inc. and Peer Music Ltd., 1975.

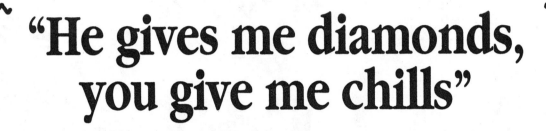

"He gives me diamonds, you give me chills"

— Don Goodman and Mary Ann Kennedy, Circle South Music and Careers-BMG Music Publishing, Inc., 1979.

"If I said you had a beautiful body, would you hold it against me?"

— David M. Bellamy, Famous Music Corp. and Bellamy Brothers Music, 1979.

"Get your biscuits in the oven and your buns in the bed"

— Kinky Friedman, Ensign Music, 1972.

Leader of the outlandish country rock band the Texas Jewboys,
Kinky Friedman once was a Peace Corps worker in Borneo.

"I hate the way I love it"

— Averal Aldridge, Big Hair Music and Song Doctor Music, 1978.
Reached No. 16 when recorded by Charly McClain and Johnny Rodriguez for Epic Records.

"Where are you spending your nights these days?"

— Steve Dorff, Snuff Garrett, Milton Brown and Harold Thorn, Private Dancer Music, 1983.
Reached No. 10 when recorded in 1983 by David Frizzell for Viva Records.

"I feel better all over more than anywhere's else"

— Leon Smith and Kenny Rogers, Central Songs Inc., 1954.
Reached No. 6 when recorded in 1955 by Ferlin Husky for Capitol Records.

"When the tingle becomes a chill"

— Lola Dillon, Tree Publishing Co. Inc., 1973.
Reached No. 2 when recorded in 1975 by Loretta Lynn for MCA Records.

"Whatcha got cookin' in your oven tonight?"

— Pat McManus and Wilson Lee Bomar, Music City Music, 1983.

"Love never hurt so good"

— Mary Fielder and Robert
Whitaker, Combine Music
and Music City Music, 1981.

"Loving here, living there and lying in between"

— Eugene Dobbins, Tony Austin and Johnny A. Wilson, Chappel and Co., and Full Swing Music, 1977.

"I still hold her body, but I think I've lost her mind"

—R. Sawyer and D. Locorriere, Horse Hairs Music Inc., 1979.

"Don't stay on your side of the bed tonight"

—Ann Morton and Eddie
Roger, Accredit Music
and One More Music, 1979.

*Reached No. 86 when recorded in
1979 by Ann Morton.*

"Frost on my roof, but there's fire in my furnace"

— Opal Jean Holmes, Acuff-Rose Music Inc., 1955.

"I'm having daydreams about night things in the middle of the afternoon"

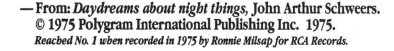

— From: *Daydreams about night things,* John Arthur Schweers.
© 1975 Polygram International Publishing Inc. 1975.
Reached No. 1 when recorded in 1975 by Ronnie Milsap for RCA Records.

"Lay something on my bed besides a blanket"

— Gladys Scaife, Ronny Scaife and Daniel Hogan, Songs of Polygram International Inc., Sherrill Music and Partner Music, 1977.

Reached No. 82 when recorded in 1977 by Charly McClain for Epic Records.

"Should I come home or should I go crazy?"

—Joe Allen, Tree Publishing Co. Inc., 1973.

"If the phone doesn't ring, it's me"

—Jimmy Buffett, Wyland Arnold Jennings and Michael E. Utley, Coral Reefer Music and Blue Sky Rider Music, 1985.

"I'm the one she missed him with today"

— Doodle Owens, Jonesongs and First Lady Songs Inc., 1981.

"I only miss you on days that end in 'Y'"

— From: *Days that end in 'Y.'* Jim
Malloy, Even Stevens. © 1975
Screen Gems-EMI Music Inc. All
rights reserved. Used by permission.

"I've cried the blue right out of my eyes"

— Loretta Lynn, Sure-Fire Music, 1970.

Reached No. 23 when recorded in 1970 by Crystal Gayle for Decca Records.

"How come your dog don't bite nobody but me?"

— Wayne Walker and Mel
Tillis, Cedarwood
Publishing and Wayne
Walker Music, 1961.

*A prolific songwriter who
once studied violin, Mel Tillis
recorded this song in a duet
with Webb Pierce that reached
No. 25 on the charts in 1963.*

"Couldn't love have picked a better place to die?"

— Curly Putman and Bucky Jones, Cross Keys Publishing, 1980.

"We used to kiss each other on the lips, but it's all over now"

—Ann Morton and Eddie Roger, Hitkit Music and Accredit Music.
Reached No. 63 when recorded in 1980 by Ann Morton.

"All I want from you is away"

— Bobby L. Harden, King Coal Music Inc., 1975.

"I've got tears in my ears from lyin' on my back in my bed while I cry over you"

— Harold Barlow, © 1949 by Leo Feist, Inc. Copyright renewed 1977 by Harold Barlow. All rights administered by Commonwealth Music Company. All rights reserved. Used by permission.

Harold Barlow's four-year-old son inspired this song when crying on his bed one day because he was indoors while the other children were playing outside.

"Not tonight, I've got a heartache"

— Walt Aldridge and Tom
Brasfield, Rick Hall
Music, 1977.

"I've enjoyed as much of this as I can stand"

— Bill Anderson, 1962. One of many songs written by Bill Anderson, who was nicknamed "Whispering Bill" because he didn't have much of a singing voice.

"Is this the best I'm gonna feel?"

— Don Gibson, Acuff-Rose Music Inc., 1972.
Reached No. 11 when recorded by Don Gibson in 1972 for Hickory Records.

"Ever since we said 'I do,' there's so many things you don't"

—Johnny Slate and Red Lane, Tree Publishing Co. Inc., 1970.

"One has my name, the other has my heart"

— Hal Blair, Eddie Dean and Lorene Dean, Anne Rachel Music Corp.
and Southern Music Publishing, 1948.

*Reached No. 3 when recorded in 1969 by Jerry Lee Lewis for Smash Records.
Co-writer Hal Blair said this song was banned by some churches.*

"It's sad to go to the funeral of a good love that has died"

— Barbara Fairchild and Randy Reinhard, Ape Leg Music, 1978.

"I gave her the ring, she gave me the finger"

— F.W. Markle, 1967.

"My tears have washed 'I love you' from the blackboard of my heart"

— From: *Blackboard of my heart,* Hank Thompson and Lyle Gaston, © 1956 Songs of Polygram International and Polygram International Publishing Inc.

"If fingerprints showed up on skin, wonder whose I'd find on you?"

— From: *If fingerprints showed up on skin*, Freddie Hart and
Kenneth E. Hunt, Blue Book Music and Ching-Ring Music, 1970.

"I don't know whether to kill myself or go bowling"

—From: *I don't know whether to kill myself,* Thomas J. Sharp, © Sharptone Productions, 1978.
Thom Sharp is a standup comic in California who likes to sing country songs as a part of his act.

Chapter 4

Drink Up

"What's made Milwaukee famous made a loser out of me"

— Glenn Sutton, Al Gallico Music, 1968.

Reached No. 2 when recorded in 1968 for Smash Records, by Jerry Lee Lewis, who has two famous cousins — country singer Mickey Gilley and TV preacher Jimmy Swaggart.

"If drinkin' don't kill me, her memory will"

— Richard Beresford and
Harlan Sanders, Warner-
Tamerlane Publishing Corp.
and Careers-BMG Music, 1981.

*Reached No. 8 when recorded in 1981
by George Jones for Epic Records.*

"If I say I love you, consider me drunk"

— Sanger D. Shafer, Acuff-Rose Publications Inc., 1980.

"Don't come home a drinkin' with lovin' on your mind"

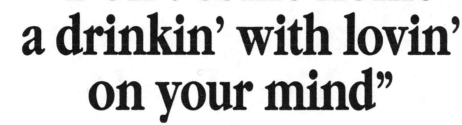

— Loretta Lynn and Peggy Wells,
Sure Fire Music Inc., 1966.

*Reached No. 1 when recorded in 1966 by
Loretta Lynn for Decca Records. Born into
poverty in Butcher's Holler, Kentucky, and
married at age fourteen, Loretta Lynn became
the first woman to win country music's
"Entertainer of the Year" award in 1972.*

"She's acting single, I'm drinking doubles"

— Wayne Carson, Budde Songs Inc. and Warner-Tamerlane Publishing Corp., 1974.

"One drink is too many, and a hundred's not enough"

— Ira Louvin and Anne Young, Acuff-Rose Music Inc., 1965.

"I'm two beers away from a beautiful day"

— From: *Two beers away*, Johnny Gimble, © 1980 Screen Gems-EMI Music Inc. All rights administered by Screen Gems-EMI Music Inc. All rights reserved. Used by permission.

"Whiskey made me stumble, the devil made me fall"

— Hugh Moffait, Bogguillas Canyon and Atlantic Music, 1981.

"Red necks, white socks and blue ribbon beer"

— Charks G. Neese, Wayland Holyfield and Robert Lee McDill,
Polygram International and Jack-Music Inc., 1973.

Chapter 5
The Devil and the Divine

"Heaven's just a sin away"

— Jerry W. Gillespie, Lorville Music Company, 1969.
Reached No. 1 when recorded in 1977 by The Kendalls for Ovation Records.

"I love that woman like the devil loves sin"

— Bucky Jones, Joane Keller and Paul Huffman, Walter A. Smith and Muhlenberg Music, 1974.

"This kinda love ain't meant for Sunday school"

— Jimmy Walker, Acuff-Rose Music Inc., 1977.

"I'm the only hell mama ever raised"

— Bobby Borchers, Wayne Kemp and Mack Vickery, Tree Publishing Co. Inc., 1975.

Reached No. 8 when recorded in 1977 by Johnny Paycheck for Epic Records.

"I don't have to die to get into heaven"

— Tim Daniels, Gene Dobbins and Tommy Rocco, Unichappel Music,
Intersong Music and Satin Pony Music, 1981.

"Drop kick me, Jesus, through the goalposts of life"

"Saturday Satan,
Sunday saint"

— Wayne Walker, Cedarwood Publishing, 1963.

"Thank God and Greyhound you're gone"

wheeew!

—From: *Thank God and Greyhound,* Larry Kingston and Ed Nix, © 1970 Careers-BMG Music Publishing, Inc. Used by permission. All rights reserved.

"You're the reason our kids are ugly"

—L.E. White and Lola Dillon, Tree Publishing Co. Inc. and Coal Miners Music, 1977.

"Old King Kong was just a little monkey compared to my love for you"

— Old King Kong, © Sammy Lyons,
Sherrill Music, 1977.

*Reached No. 34 when recorded in 1977
by George Jones for Epic Records.*

"Worst you ever gave me was the best I ever had"

— Daniel D. Hice and Ruby F. Hice, Mandy Music, 1976.

"The future is not what it used to be"

— Mickey Newbury, Acuff-Rose Publications, 1977.

"If I don't love you, grits ain't groceries"

— George Jones, Fort Knox Music, Inc., Trio Music Co., Inc., Glad Music Co., 1959.

George Jones has influenced more country singers than perhaps anyone else alive. His first big hit was "Why Baby Why" in 1955.

"Waitin' in your welfare line"

—Buck Owens, Don Rich and Nat Stuckey, Tree Publishing Co. Inc., 1966.
Reached No. 1 when recorded in 1966 by Buck Owens for Capitol Records.

"If loving you is wrong, I don't want to be right"

— Raymond Jackson, Carl Hampton and Homer Banks, Irving Music Inc., 1972.
Reached No. 1 when recorded in 1979 by Barbara Mandrell for ABC Records.

"I miss you already and you're not even gone"

— Marvin Rainwater and Faron Young, Tree Publishing Co. Inc., 1956.

"Married, but not to each other"

— Ora Craig and Frances Miller, Bridgeport Music, 1975.
Reached No. 3 when recorded in 1977 by Barbara Mandrell for ABC Records.

"Why don't you haul off and love me?"

— Wayne Raney and
Lonnie Glossen, Fort
Knox Music Co., 1964.

"Truth is, we're livin' a lie"

— John Bettis and R.C. Bannon, Warner-Tamerlane Publishing Corp. and WB Music Corp., 1978.

"My shoes keep walking back to you"

—James Robert Wills and Lee Ross,
Copar Music Inc., and Chappell
and Co. Inc., 1958.

"That's more about love than I wanted to know"

— Dickey Lee, Robert Lee McDill and Bucky E. Jones, Hall-Clement Publishing and Cross Keys Publishing, 1984.

Reached No. 49 when recorded in 1986 by Nicolette Larson for MCA Records.

"She left love all over me"

— Chester Lester, Warner
House of Music, 1982.

"This time I've hurt her more than she loves me"

— Earl Thomas Conley and Mary Smoot Larkin, Blue Moon Music and Zomba Enterprises, 1975.

"I'm ashamed to be here, but not ashamed enough to leave"

—From: *I'm ashamed to be here*, Jack Butcher and John Martin, © Adventure Music, 1974.

"You can eat crackers in my bed anytime"

— Title: *Crackers*, Kye Fleming and Dennis W. Morgan, © 1980 Pi-Gem Music Inc.
Reached No. 3 when recorded in 1980 by Barbara Mandrell for MCA Records.

"You snap your fingers and I'm back in your hands"

— John Schweers, Chess Music, Inc., 1976.

Have you got a favorite line from a country song? Are you sure it's legitimate? Some of the funniest lines often turn out to be fabricated. Send your best, along with the title of the song it's from and the name of the songwriter and the publisher, to:

Best Country Lines
c/o Andrews and McMeel
4900 Main Street
Kansas City, Missouri 64112

A portion of the proceeds from this book will be donated to NSAI, the Nashville Songwriters Association International, a not-for-profit group that promotes songwriters who often toil without recognition.